D1561098

DIDO AND AENEAS

in Full Score

Henry Purcell

Edited by
William H. Cummings

DOVER PUBLICATIONS, INC.
New York

Bibliographical Note

This Dover edition, first published in 1995, is an unabridged, corrected republication of the work originally published in an authoritative English edition, n.d. [1915]. The Dover edition adds a full list of credits and characters; editorial notes about the notation of the Sorceress' music and concerning the work's instrumentation; a revised list of contents; and corrections in the marginal matter (instrumentation, headings).

Library of Congress Cataloging-in-Publication Data

Purcell, Henry, 1659–1695.
    Dido and Aeneas / Henry Purcell ; edited by William H. Cummings.—In full score.
    1 score.
    Opera in 3 acts.
    Libretto by Nahum Tate.
    Based on: Aeneid / Virgil.
    Originally published: London : Novello, 1915?
    ISBN 0-486-28746-7
    1. Operas—Scores.   2. Dido (Legendary character)—Drama.   3. Aeneas (Legendary character)—Drama.   I. Cummings, William Hayman, 1831–1915.   II. Tate, Nahum, 1652–1715.   III. Virgil. Aeneis.   IV. Title.
M1500.P98D5   1995 ‹Case›   95-22550
                                                                            CIP
                                                                            M

Manufactured in the United States of America
Dover Publications, Inc., 31 East 2nd Street, Mineola, N.Y. 11501

DIDO AND AENEAS

OPERA IN A PROLOGUE AND THREE ACTS
Libretto by Nahum Tate
Music by Henry Purcell

First performance [?]: 1680? 1689?
"An Opera Perform'd
at Mr. Josias Priest's Boarding-School
at Chelsey. By Young Gentlewomen."

CHARACTERS

Dido, *Queen of Carthage* . . . . Soprano

Belinda, *Dido's lady in waiting* . . . . Soprano

Woman ["2nd Woman"/"Attendant"] . . . . Soprano

Two Witches* . . . . Sopranos

Spirit, *a false messenger* . . . . Soprano

Aeneas, *Prince of Troy* . . . . Tenor

1st Sailor . . . . Tenor

Sorceress . . . . Bass**

Chorus (SATB):
Courtiers, Hunting Party, Witches,
Furies ["Fairies"?], Sailors and Their Women, Cupids

Setting: Carthage and vicinity in Antiquity

*called "Inchanteresses" in the libretto

**Except for No. 30 (pp. 70–2), the Sorceress' music is notated as a "Bass" part,
but well within the baritone range

In No. 30, without explanation, the same part is notated in the treble clef,
still labelled "Bass," within the range

INSTRUMENTATION

This edition calls for a small chamber ensemble of two violins, viola and "basso," with a fully notated keyboard realization of the continuo's figured bass. "We can well imagine that the space available at Mr. Priest's boarding-school made the scanty orchestration a necessity . . ." [from the Preface].

The written-out harpsichord part* was William H. Cummings' contribution—along with other editorial additions—for his 1889 edition of Purcell's work. No such realization was provided in the first edition of *Dido and Aeneas*, published by The Musical Antiquarian Society, London, in 1841.

*anachronistically labelled PIANO throughout [at a later date?], but corrected in the Dover edition

CONTENTS

ACT II.

SCENE: THE GROVE.

ACT III.

SCENE: THE SHIPS.

THE END.

DIDO AND ÆNEAS.

PREFACE.

T has long been generally believed that Purcell composed the opera "Dido and Æneas" when only nineteen years of age, and although there can be little doubt that Purcell's genius was fully equal to such a task, the fact remains that he was twenty-two years old when called upon to provide the music of this opera for a special occasion. The erroneous belief was first promulgated by Sir John Hawkins in his "History of Music," where we find the following statement:— "One, Mr. Josias Priest, a celebrated dancing master and a composer of stage dances, kept a boarding-school for young gentlewomen in Leicester Fields. The nature of his profession inclining him to dramatic representations, he got Tate to write, and Purcell to set to music, a little drama called 'Dido and Æneas.' Purcell was then of the age of nineteen, but the music of this opera had so little the appearance of a puerile essay, that there was scarce a musician in England who would not have thought it an honour to have been the author of it. The exhibition of this little piece by the young gentlewomen of the school, to a select audience of their parents and friends, was attended with general applause, no small part of which was considered as the due of Purcell."* The above narration of Hawkins has been generally accepted as correct, and we find it quoted in the Preface written by Professor Taylor for an edition of the opera published by the "Musical Antiquarian Society" in 1841. Mr. Husk has varied the Hawkins story in his article on Purcell in Grove's "Dictionary of Music," where he says, "In 1675, when only seventeen years of age, Purcell wrote the music to 'Dido and Æneas'"; and "the music was *again* performed in 1680," but he does not support his new theory by any evidence or authority.

We may note that Dr. Burney's "History of Music" does not contain any reference to "Dido and Æneas"—all the evidence hitherto discovered tends to prove that the opera was composed in 1680. The *London Gazette*, November 25, 1680, has the following advertisement: "Josias Priest, dancing master, who kept a school of gentlewomen in Leicester Fields, is removed to the Great School House at Chelsey, that was Mr. Portman's. There will continue the same masters, and others, to the improvement of the said School." The library of the Sacred Harmonic Society, now happily preserved in the Royal College of Music, contains an original libretto of the opera, believed to be unique,† with the following title: "An opera perform'd at Mr. Josias Priest's boarding-school at Chelsey by young gentlewomen. The words made by Mr. Nat. Tate.‡ The musick composed by Mr. Henry Purcell."

In D'Urfey's "New Poems," an octavo volume published in 1690, there is the following: "Epilogue to the opera of 'Dido and Æneas,' performed at Mr. Priest's boarding-school at Chelsey. Spoken by the Lady Dorothy Burk."

> " All that we know the Angels do above,
> I've read, is that they Sing and that they love,
> The Vocal part we have to night perform'd
> And if by Love our Hearts not yet are warm'd
> Great Providence has still more bountious been
> To save us from those grand Deceivers Men.
> Here blest with Innocence, and peace of Mind, ⎫
> Not only bred to Virtue, but inclin'd ;   ⎬
> We flowrish, and defie all human kind.   ⎭

---

* Vol. IV., p. 49, original quarto ed. Hawkins's "History of Music." Vol. II., p. 745, Novello's Edition.
† A fac-simile of this libretto is by permission prefixed to this edition of the Opera.
‡ *Nat.* is doubtless a misprint for *Nah.* (Nahum).

Art's curious Garden thus we learn to know,
And here secure from nipping Blasts we grow,
Let the vain Fop range o'er yon vile lewd Town,
Learn Play-house Wit, and vow 'tis all his own ;
Let him Cock, Huff, Strut, Ogle, Lye, and Swear,
How he's admir'd by such and such a Player ;
All 's one to us, his Charms have here no power,
Our Hearts have just the Temper as before ;
Besides to shew we live with strictest Rules,
Our Nunnery-Door is charm'd to shut out Fools ;
No Love-toy here can pass to private view,
Nor *China* Orange cram'd with Billet dew,
Rome may allow strange Tricks to please her Sons,
But we are Protestants and English Nuns,
Like nimble Fawns, and Birds that bless the Spring
Unscar'd by turning Times we dance and sing ;
We in hope to please, but if some Critick here
Fond of his Wit, designs to be severe,
Let not his Patience be worn out too soon,
And in few years we shall be all in Tune."

This doggrel written by Tom d'Urfey was evidently recited by one of the young gentlewomen of the school, and as she was Lady Dorothy Burk, we may infer that Mr. Priest's pupils were of the aristocratic class.

Priest was not only " a celebrated dancing master and composer of dances for the stage," but appears also to have been professionally attached to the theatre in *Dorset Gardens ;* we find his name specially recorded in connection with the production of " Macbeth " as altered by Davenant ; also for " King Arthur," " The Prophetess," " The Fairy Queen," plays for which Purcell composed the music. A reference to the original libretto of " Dido and Æneas " will show that Tate was not forgetful of Mr. Priest's professional avocations, every opportunity for introducing a dance being carefully utilised.

The music of " Dido and Æneas " remained in MS. until 1841, when an edition was published by " The Musical Antiquarian Society," with prefaces by Professor Taylor and Mr. G. A. Macfarren. No libretto of the work was known at that time, and Macfarren wrote : " Unable to meet with a copy of the drama separate from the music, and the MS. scores to which I have had access presenting but the mere words and the names of the characters who sing them, I have ventured to make such divisions of the Acts as were suggested to me by apparent musical climaxes and by the progress of the plot." In 1870 Dr. Rimbault published an edition of the opera in vocal score ; the libretto had then been discovered, and the Doctor availed himself of the opportunity of consulting it, with the result that he noted the omission of several pieces of music in the Antiquarian Society edition, but after diligent search failed to discover the missing music in the various MSS. he was able to consult. He therefore adopted the Act divisions which Macfarren had suggested.

A few years since I was so fortunate as to secure a MS. score of the opera, written probably in Purcell's time, and also an old set of instrumental and vocal parts which had been used in performance. These I have collated with a fine MS. score written by John Travers,* about 1720, kindly placed at my disposal by the Rev. Sir F. A. G. Ouseley. The MSS. supply the missing music,† now first printed in complete score. It is worthy of remark that the whole of the solo parts, excepting that for the tenor, *Æneas,* are written with the G clef, a significant reminder that the music was composed for performance by " Young Gentlewomen." *Dido's* attendant is named *Belinda,* agreeing with the printed libretto. A remark made by Sir John Hawkins would lead us to believe that he had never seen an authentic copy of the opera. He says : " The song in the ' Orpheus Britannicus,' ' Ah, Belinda,' is one of the airs in it (' Dido and Æneas '). In the original opera the initial words are ' Ah, my Anna ! ' " My own and the Rev. Sir F. A. G. Ouseley's scores give various stage directions, marks of time and expression—these are few and always in English. To these others are now added, in Italian, to distinguish them from Purcell's.

Professor Taylor, in his Preface to " Dido," speaks of the surprising originality of Purcell, of his quick and accurate perception of the use and power of music regarded as a dramatic agent ; these qualities are very discernible in the recently discovered MS. scores of the opera, for we find that Purcell made many of his scenes continuous ; in this, as in other details, showing himself far in advance of his age and contemporaries. In producing a perfect

---

* Travers, an excellent musician and composer, was originally a chorister in St. George's Chapel, Windsor, afterward a pupil of Dr. Greene and Dr. Pepusch ; the latter bequeathed to him one half of his large and valuable library. Travers was Organist of the Chapel Royal at the time of his decease, 1758. He was then about 55 years of age.

† Purcell probably did not set the Prologue to music. We know that on other occasions he exercised similar discretion in the treatment of stage dramas.

opera, without spoken dialogue, but including recitative, air, duet, chorus, and descriptive instrumental movements, he had no model to work upon. It is true that Sir William Davenant gave a performance or entertainment at Rutland House* on the 21st of May, 1656, described by Wood† as an Italian Opera. Hawkins refers to Wood's statement, which he says "is much to be doubted." As a matter of fact, the description was most inaccurate. The entertainment was published in a small octavo volume, probably on November 21, 1656, but with the printed date 1657. A copy of this rare little book is in my own library.‡ It is evident that the entertainment consisted chiefly of long-spoken monologues, divided by instrumental music. There are only two vocal pieces—songs with chorus—in the whole work. It is entirely in English, not Italian. This seems to have been a trial venture of Davenant to re-introduce stage representations, which had been sternly repressed by the Puritans. He soon attempted a more lengthened and a more dramatic entertainment, "The Siege of Rhodes." This may have been performed in 1656, but probably in the following year 1657. The libretto was published in August, 1656, and it is evident from the address " to the Reader," prefixed to the work, that at the time of publication it had not been performed. In a letter addressed by Davenant to Sir Bulstrode Whitelock, the Lord-Keeper, dated September 3, 1656, he says: "When I consider the nicety of the times, I fear it may draw a curtain between your Lordship and our Opera; therefore I have presumed to send your Lordship, hot from the press, what we mean to represent, making your Lordship my supreme judge, though I despair to have the honour of inviting you to be a spectator." There can be no doubt that Davenant adopted the title *Opera* for his entertainments because he dared not call them stage plays, and for like reason he made them as musical as possible. When at length he found the authorities and the public ready to tolerate plays and tragedies without music he continued to call them operas. Sir G. Macfarren, in " Musical History," says the " Siege of Rhodes " was a regular opera, and retained the stage until some years after the Restoration, and adduces this statement as a refutation of the commonly-received opinion that Puritan influence brought about a decadence of music in England. This inference is scarcely warranted by facts. The first edition (1656) of the " Siege of Rhodes " is full of interest, and describes with minute detail every circumstance connected with its performance, even the very size of the stage (11 feet high, 15 feet deep), the various scenes, &c.

The several characters in the piece delivered their lines in a sort of monotone or chant, described by Aubrey in his " Miscellanies," as "*stilo recitativo*," and referred to by Dryden, who says "the 'Siege of Rhodes' was the first opera we ever had in England; there is this difference between opera and tragedy, that the one is a story sung with proper action, the other spoken. He must be a very ignorant player who knows not there is a musical cadence in speaking, and that a man may as well speak out of tune as sing out of tune."

The "Siege of Rhodes" was enlarged to nearly double its size within three years of its first publication, and transformed into a play; subsequently the author made further additions, and it was in this altered state that it " retained the stage after the Restoration." The music for the first representation of the " Siege of Rhodes " was composed by Henry Lawes, Captain Henry Cook, Matthew Lock, Dr. Charles Colman, and Mr. George Hudson, but it is significant that none of the music has survived to our times.

Purcell's predecessors, Lawes, Laniere, Locke, and Banister had each written detached recitatives, but none of them had attempted the composition of a perfect opera, and it is curious that not one of Purcell's contemporaries, with the exception of Lewis Grabu, followed the model given in " Dido and Æneas." Grabu, in 1687, set to music Dryden's opera " Albion and Albanius," entirely discarding spoken dialogue. This work is sometimes erroneously cited as the *first* opera performed in England; it had no success, and if we couple this fact with the recollection that Purcell himself never produced another opera, we may conclude that the times were not then ripe for true music-drama or opera.

The choruses in " Dido and Æneas " are remarkable for their melodiousness and suitableness for stage purposes. The number commencing " In our deep vaulted cell " was evidently performed by two sets of singers, one in view of the audience and the other behind the scenes, an effective novelty, which must have been a delightful surprise at the first representation of the opera. The final chorus is particularly beautiful, forming an appropriate close to *Dido's* death scene, in which she sings one of the most pathetic songs ever composed. In this song, as in numerous other numbers in the work, the composer voluntarily fettered his genius by composing his melodies and harmonies to a ground-bass. This learned device

---

* Rutland House was situate at the North-east corner of Charterhouse Square.
† Athen. Oxon. Vol. II., col. 412.
‡ "The first Day's Entertainment at Rutland House, by Declamations and Musick; After the manner of the Ancients, By Sir W. D. London: Printed by J. M. for H. Herringman, and sold at his shop at the Anchor, in the New-Exchange, in the Lower Walk. 1657."

was a favourite one with Purcell, and it is curious to note that the ground of *Dido's* song is nearly identical with that afterward used by J. S. Bach to the " Crucifixus " in his B minor Mass.

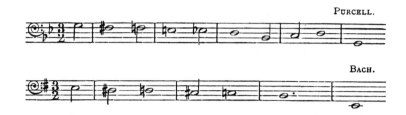

Purcell's original orchestration is for two violins, viola, bass, and harpsichord. Some of the recitatives are accompanied by the stringed orchestra, in other cases the recitatives and also some of the airs have an accompaniment for the harpsichord alone. We can well imagine that the space available at Mr. Priest's boarding-school made the scanty orchestration a necessity in this particular instance; in other works composed for the theatre Purcell sometimes wrote for *three* hautboys, trumpets, bassoons, and drums. Dr. Rimbault hazarded a conjecture that the part of *Belinda* was written for a male alto, and that at the first performance the composer, who possessed a beautiful alto voice, and was an accomplished vocalist, sang and performed it himself. The discovery of the MSS. from which this edition has been prepared has dissipated that myth; *Belinda's* part is written for a high soprano, and it is far more probable that Purcell presided at the harpsichord, and supplied the necessary filling up accompaniment. What that was like it is impossible to say, but, judging from harmonies and progressions which we find in Purcell's music,* we may be quite sure that it was replete with fancy and beauty.

The author of the libretto, Nahum Tate, born in Dublin in 1652, is chiefly remembered as the co-author with Nicholas Brady of a metrical version of the Psalms of David. He was associated with Purcell on several other occasions in the production of odes and pieces for the stage.

"Dido and Æneas" was occasionally performed at "The Ancient Concerts," also by the old "Purcell Society," and recently revived by the "Bach Choir," when the music was performed as here printed. Some of the pieces have at times been divorced from the work and introduced into stage plays, without regard to their appropriateness; for example, "Fear no danger" was thrust into Shakespeare's "Measure for Measure," as may be seen from a copy of the music of the duet published in 1700.

WILLIAM H. CUMMINGS.

* The Motet "Jehovah quam multo," published for the Bach Choir, by Novello should be examined by all who are interested in Purcell and his wondrous harmonies.

DIDO AND AENEAS

AN OPERA

Perform'd at
Mr. JOSIAS PRIEST's Boarding-School at
CHELSEY.
By Young Gentlewomen.
The Words Made by Mr. NAT. TATE.
The Mufick Compofed by Mr. **Henry Purcell.**

The PROLOGUE.

Phœbus Rifes in the Chariot,
Over the Sea, The *Nereids* out of the Sea.

Phœbus,   FRom *Aurora's* Spicy Bed,
        Phœbus rears his Sacred Head.
His Courfers Advancing,
Curvetting and Prancing.

1. *Nereid, Phœbus* ftrives in vain to Tame 'em,
    With *Ambrofia* Fed too high.

2. *Nereid, Phœbus* ought not now to blame 'em,
    Wild and eager to Survey
    The faireft Pageant of the Sea.

Phœbus,   *Tritons* and *Nereids* come pay your Devotion

Cho.   To the New rifing Star of the Ocean.
        Venus Defcends in her Chariot,
        The *Tritons* out of the Sea,
        The Tritons Dance.

Nereid,   Look down ye Orbs and See
    A New Divinity.

Phœ.   Whofe Luftre does Out-Shine
Your fainter Beams, and half Eclipfes mine,
Give *Phœbus* leave to Prophecy.
Phœbus all Events can fee.
Ten Thoufand Thoufand Harmes,
From fuch prevailing Charmes,
To Gods and Men muft inftantly Enfue.

Cho.   And if the Deity's above,
Are *Victims* of the powers of Love,
What muft wretched Mortals do.

Venus)   Fear not *Phœbus,* fear not me,
    A harmlefs Deity.

Thefe

These are all my Guards ye View.
What can thefe blind Archers do.

Phœ.   Blind they are, but ftrike the Heart,

Ven.   What *Phœbus* fay's is alwayes true.
They Wound indeed, but 'tis a pleafing fmart.

Phœ.   Earth and Skies addrefs their Duty,
To the Sovereign Queen of Beauty.
          All Refigning,
          None Repining
At her undifputed Sway.

Cho,   To *Phœbus* and *Venus* our Homage wee'l pay,
Her Charmes bleft the Night, as his Beams bleft the day.
       The Nereids Dance.   *Exit.)*

    The Spring Enters with her Nymphs. [*Scene the Grove.*

Ven.   See the Spring in all her Glory,

Cho,   Welcomes *Venus* to the Shore.

Ven.   Smiling Hours are now before you,
Hours that may return no more. [*Exit, Phœ. Ven. Soft Mufick*

Spring,   Our Youth and Form declare,
For what we were defigned.
'Twas Nature made us Fair,
And you muft make us kind.
He that fails of Addreffing,
'Tis but Juft he fhould fail of Poffeffing.
     The Spring and Nymphs Dance.

Shepherdeffes, Jolly Shepherds come away.
To Celebrate this Genial Day,
And take the Friendly Hours you vow to pay.
 Now make Trial,
 And take no Denial.
Now carry your Game, or for ever give o're.
    The Shepherds and Shepherdeffes Dance.

Cho.   Let us Love and happy Live,
Poffefs thofe fmiling Hours,
The more aufpicious Powers,
And gentle Planets give.
Prepare thofe foft returns to Meet,
That makes Loves Torments Sweet.
      The Nymphs Dance.

                  Enter

Enter the Country Shepherds and Shepherdeſſes.

He, Tell, Tell me, prithee *Dolly*,
And leave thy Melancholy,
Why on the Plaines, the Nymphs and Swaines,
This Morning are ſo Jolly.

She, By *Zephires* gentle Blowing,
And *Venus* Graces Flowing,
The Sun has bin to Court our Queen,
And Tired the Spring with wooing.

He, The Sun does guild our Bowers,

She, The Spring does yield us Flowers,
She ſends the Vine,

He, He makes the Wine,
To Charm our happy Hours.

She, She gives our Flocks their Feeding,

He, He makes 'em fit for Breeding.

She, She decks the Plain,

He, He fills the Grain,
And makes it worth the Weeding.

Cho, But the Jolly Nymph *Thitis* that long his Love ſought,
Has Fluſtred him now with a large Morning's draught.
Let's go and divert him, whilſt he is Mellow,
You know in his Cups he's a Hot-Headed Fellow.
The Countrys Maids Dance.   [*Exit.*

A C T the Firſt,
Scene the Palace
Enter *Dido* and *Belinda,* and *Train.*

Bel. SHake the Cloud from off your Brow,
Fate your wiſhes do Allow.
Empire Growing,
Pleaſures Flowing,
Fortune Smiles and ſo ſhould you,
Shake the Cloud from off your Brow,

Cho. Baniſh Sorrow, Baniſh Care,
Grief ſhould ne're approach the Fair.

Dido, Ah! *Belinda* I am preſt,
With Torment not to be Confeſt.
Peace and I are Strangers grown,
I Languiſh till my Grief is known,
Yet wou'd not have it Gueſt.
Grief

Bel.	Grief Encreaſing, by Concealing,
Dido	Mine admits of no Revealing.
Bel.	Then let me Speak the *Trojan* gueſt,
	Into your tender Thoughts has preſt.
2 *Women*,	The greateſt bleſſing Fate can give,
	Our *Carthage* to ſecure, and *Troy* revive.
Cho.	VVhen Monarchs unite how happy their State,
	They Triumph at once on their Foes and their Fate.
Dido,	VVhence could ſo much Virtue Spring,
	VVhat Stormes, what Battels did he Sing.
	Anchiſes Valour mixt with *Venus's* Charmes,
	How ſoft in Peace, and yet how fierce in Armes.
Bel.	A Tale ſo strong and full of wo,
	Might melt the Rocks as well as you.
2 *Women*,	VVhat ſtubborn Heart unmoved could ſee,
	Such Diſtreſs, ſuch pity.
Dido,	Mine with Stormes of Care oppreſt,
	Is Taught to pity the Diſtreſt.
	Mean wretches grief can Touch,
	So ſoft ſo ſenſible my Breaſt,
	But Ah ! I fear, I pity his too much.
Bel.	Fear no danger to Enſue,
2 *Women*,	The *Hero* Loves as well as you.
Cho.	Ever Gentle, ever Smiling,
	And the Cares of Life beguiling.
	Cupid Strew your path with Flowers,
	Gathered from *Elizian* Bowers.

Dance this Cho.

The Baske.

Æneas *Enters with his Train.*

Bel.	See your Royal Gueſt appears,
	How God like is the Form he bears.
Æn.	VVhen Royal Fan ſhall I be bleſt,
	VVith cares of Love, and State diſtreſt.
Dido.	Fate forbids what you Enſue,
	Æneas has no Fate but, you.
	Let *Dido* Smile, and I'le defie,
	The Feeble ſtroke of Deſtiny.

Cupid

Cho.	*Cupid* ony throws the Dart.
	That's dreadful to a Warriour's Heart.
	And fhe that VVounds can only cure the Smart.
Æn.	If not for mine, for Empire's fake,
	Some pity on your Lover take.
	Ah ! make not in a hopelefs Fire,
	A *Hero* fall, and *Troy* once more Empire.
Bel.	Pursue thy Conqueft, Love—her Eyes,
	Confefs the Flame her Tongue Denyes.

A Dance Gittars Chacony

Cho.	To the Hills and the Vales, to the Rocks and the Mountains
	To the Mufical Groves, and the cool Shady Fountains.
	Let the Triumphs of Love and of Beauty be Shown,
	Go Revel ye *Cupids*, the day is your own.

The Triumphing Dance.

ACT the Second,

Scene the Cave.
Enter *Sorcerefs.*

Sorc.	WEyward Sifters you that Fright,
	The Lonely Traveller by Night.
	VVho like difmal Ravens Crying,
	Beat the VVindowes of the Dying.
	Appear at my call, and fhare in the Fame,
	Of a Mifchief fhall make all *Carthage* to Flame.

Enter Inchanterefses.

Incha.	Say *Beldam* what's thy will,
	Harms our Delight and Mifchief all our Skill,
Sorc.	The Queen of *Carthage* whom we hate,
	As we do all in profperous State.
	E're Sun fet fhall moft wretched prove,
	Deprived of Fame, of Life and Love.
Cho.	Ho, ho, ho, ho, ho, ho, &c.
Incha.	Ruin'd e're the Set of Sun,
	Tell us how fhall this be done.
Sorc.	The *Trojan* Prince you know is bound
	By Fate to feek *Italian* Ground,
	The Queen and He are now in Chafe,
	Hark, how the cry comes on apace.
	But when they've done, my trufty Elf
	In form of *Mercury* himself.
	As fent from *Jove* fhall chide his ftay,
	And Charge him Sail to Night with all his Fleet away.
	Ho, Ho, ho, ho, &c. [*Enter 2 Drunken Saylors, a Dance*

But

xix

Sorc.	But e're we, we this perform.
	We'l Conjure for a Storm
	To Mar their Hunting Sport,
	And drive 'em back to Court.
Cho.	In our deep-Vaulted Cell the Charm wee'l prepare,
	Too dreadful a Practice for this open Air,

Eccho Dance.
Inchanteresses and Fairees.

Enter Æneas, Dido and Belinda, and their Train.
Scene the Grove.

Bel.	Thanks to these Lovesome Vailes,
Cho.	These desert Hills and Dales.
	So fair the Game, so rich the Sport,
	Diana's self might to these Woods Resort.

Gitter Ground a Dance.

2d. Wom.	Oft she Visits this Loved Mountain,
	Oft she bathes her in this Fountain.
	Here *Acteon* met his Fate,
	Pursued by his own Hounds,
	And after Mortal Wounds.
	Discovered, discovered too late.

A Dance to Entertain Æneas, by Dido Vemon.

Æneas,	Behold upon my bending Spear,
	A Monsters Head stands bleeding.
	VVith Tushes far exceeding,
	These did *Venus* Huntsmen Tear.
Dido.	The Skies are Clouded, heark how Thunder
	Rends the Mountain Oaks asunder.
	Hast, hast, to Town this open Field,
	No Shelter from the Storm can yield. [Exit.

{ *The Spirit of the Sorceress descends*
{ *to Æneas in likness of* Mercury.

Spir.	Stay Prince and hear great *Joves* Command,
	He summons thee this Night away.
Æn.	To Night.
Spir.	To Night thou must forsake this Land,
	The Angry God will brook no longer stay,
	Joves Commands thee waft no more,
	In Loves delights those precious Hours,
	Allowed by the Almighty Powers.
	To gain th' *Hesperian* Shore,
	And Ruined *Troy* restore.
Æn.	*Joves* Commands shall be Obey'd,
	To Night our Anchors shall be weighed,

But

But ah ! what Language can I try,
My Injured Queen to pacify.
No fooner fhe refignes her Heart,
But from her Armes I'm forc't to part.
How can fo hard a Fate be took,
One Night enjoy'd, the next forfook.
Your be the blame, ye Gods, for I
Obey your will-but with more Eafe cou'd dye.

The Sorcerefs and her Inchanterefs.

Cho. Then fince our Charmes have Sped,
A Merry Dance be Led
By the Nymphs of *Carthage* to pleafe us.
They fhall all Dance to eafe us.
A Dance that fhall make the Spheres to wonder,
Rending thofe fair Groves afunder.

The Groves Dance.

ACT the Third,

Scene the Ships.

Enter *the Saylors.*

The Sorcerefs and her Inchanterefs.

Cho. COme away, fellow Saylors your Anchors be
Time and Tide will admit no delaying. (weighing,
Take a Bouze fhort leave of your Nymphs on the Shore,
And Silence their Morning,
VVith Vows of returning.
But never intending to Vifit them more.

The Saylors Dance.

Sorc. See the Flags and Streamers Curling,
Anchors weighing, Sails unfurling.
Phœbus pale deluding Beames,
Guilding more deceitful Streams.
Our Plot has took,
The Queen forfook, ho, ho, ho.
Elifas ruin'd, ho, ho, ho, next Motion,
Muft be to ftorme her Lover on the Ocean.
From the Ruines of others our pleafure we borrow,
Elifas bleeds to Night, and *Carthage* Flames tomorrow.

Cho. Deftruction our delight, delight our greateft Sorrow,
Elifas dyes to Night, and *Carthage* Flames to Morrow.

{Jack *of the* Lanthorn *leads the* Spaniards
{*out of their way among the Inchanteresses.*
A Dance.

Enter

Enter Dido, Belinda, *and Train.*

Dido   Your Councel all is urged in vain,
To Earth and Heaven I will Complain.
To Earth and Heaven why do I call,
Earth and Heaven confpire my Fall.
To Fate I Sue, of other means bereft,
The only refuge for the wretched left.

Bel.   See Madam where the Prince appears,
Such Sorrow in his Looks he bears, [*Æneas* Enters

Æn.   As wou'd convince you ftill he's true,
What fhall loft *Æneas* do.
How Royal fair fhall I impart,
The Gods decree and tell you we muft part.

Dido   Thus on the fatal Banks of *Nile*,
Weeps the deceitful Crocodile.
Thus Hypocrites that Murder Act,
Make Heaven and Gods the Authors of the Fact.

Æn.   By all that's good,

Dido   By all that's good no more,
All that's good you have Forfworn.
To your promifed Empire fly,
And let forfaken *Dido* dye.

Æn.   In fpite of *Joves* Command I ftay,
Offend the Gods, and Love obey.

Dido   No faithlefs Man thy courfe purfue,
I'm now refolved as well as you.
No Repentance fhall reclaim,
The Injured *Dido* flighted Flame.
For 'tis enough what e're you now decree,
That you had once a thought of leaving me.

Æn.   Let *Jove* fay what he will I'le ftay.

Dido.   Away   [*Exit Æn.*
To Death I'le fly, if longer you delay.
But Death, alas? I cannot Shun,
Death muft come when he is gone.

Cho.   Great minds againft themfelves Confpire,
And fhun the Cure they moft defire.

Dido.   Thy Hand *Belinda,* - darknefs fhades me, (*Cupids* appear in the
      On thy Bofom let me reft,   (Clouds o're her Tomb.
More I wou'd but Death invades me.
Death is now a Welcom Gueft,
When I am laid in Earth my wrongs Create.
        No trouble in thy Breaft,
         Remember me, but ah! forget my Fate.

Cho.   With drooping Wings you *Cupids* come,
To fcatter Rofes on her Tomb.
Soft and Gentle as her Heart,
Keep here your Watch and never part.   [*Cupids Dance.*
          FINIS.

OVERTURE.

ACT I.

Scene. *The Palace. Enter Dido, Belinda, and train.*

№ 1. SCENA and CHORUS.

6

№ 2. SONG.

8

№ **3**. RECIT.

№ 4. CHORUS.

12

№ 5. RECIT.

Soprano.

Basso.

Harpsichord.

Whence could so much vir-tue spring? What storms, _____ what bat-tles did he

sing? An-chi-ses' va - - - lour mixt with Ve-nus' charms, How soft, _ how

soft _ in peace, and yet how fierce, _____ how fierce in arms? A tale so

strong and full of woe Might melt _ the rocks as well as you. What

stub-born heart un-mov'd__ could see Such dis-tress, such pi-e-ty? Mine with

storms_____ of care__ op-prest Is taught to pi--ty the dis-

-trest. Mean wretch-es grief can touch So soft, so sen-si-ble my

breast; But ah! but ah! I fear I pi-ty him too much.

№ **6.** DUET and CHORUS.

16

18

Æneas enters with his train.

№ 7. RECIT.

Soprano.
BELINDA.
See, see, your Roy-al guest ap-pears; How God-like is the form he

Basso.

Harpsichord.

ÆNEAS.
bears! When, when, Roy-al fair, shall I be blest, With cares of love and state dis-

con 8^{ve} bassa

DIDO.   ÆNEAS.
-trest? Fate for-bids what you pur-sue. Æ-ne-as has no fate but you!

Let Di-do smile and I'll de-fy The fee - -ble stroke of des-ti-ny.

20

Nº 8. CHORUS.

№ 9. RECIT.

№ 10. AIR.

flame,_____ her tongue de-nies, Pur-sue thy con-quest, love, pur-sue thy con-quest,

love, pur-sue, pur-sue,_____ pur-sue thy con-quest, pur-sue thy con-quest,

love, pursue thy conquest, love, pur-sue thy conquest, love, pur-sue thy conquest, love.

№ 11. CHORUS.

Allegro assai.

- umphs, let the tri - - - - umphs of love and of beau - ty be shewn,

tri - - - - umphs, the tri-umphs of love and of beau-ty be shewn,

- umphs, let the tri-umphs, the tri-umphs of love and of beau-ty be shewn,

tri - umphs, the tri - - - umphs of love and of beau - ty be shewn,

let the tri - - - umphs, let the

let the tri-umphs, the tri - - -

let the tri - - - umphs, let the

let the tri-umphs, let the tri-umphs, the

№ 12. THE TRIUMPHING DANCE.

(At the end of the Dance thunder and lightning.)

Scene. *The Cave. Enter Sorceress.*

Nº 13. PRELUDE FOR THE WITCHES.

Wayward sisters, you that fright The lone-ly travel-ler by

con 8vé bassa.

night, Who, like dis - mal ra - vens cry - ing, Beat the win-dows of __ the dy - ing, Ap -

-pear! appear at my call, and share in the fame Of a mis-chief shall make all __ Carthage

(Enter several witches.)

1st WITCH.

flame. Appear! ap-pear! appear! ap-pear! Say, Beldame, say, what's thy will.

con 8ᵛᵉ bassa.

Nº 14. WITCHES' CHORUS.

№ **15**. RECIT.

SORCERESS.

The Queen of Carthage, whom we hate, As we do all in prosp'rous state, Ere

sun-set, shall most wretch-ed prove, Depriv'd of fame, of life and

№ 16. CHORUS.

Allegro vivace.

38

№ 17. RECIT.

done, my trus-ty Elf,___ In form of Mer-cu-ry him-self As sent from Jove, shall

chide___ his stay, And charge___ him sail to-night___ with all his fleet a-

№ 18. CHORUS.

Allegro vivace.

Nº 19. DUET.

№ 20. CHORUS. (*In the manner of an echo.*)

Nº 21. ECHO DANCE OF FURIES.

Thunder and lightning, horrid music. The Furies sink down in the cave, the rest fly up.

End of the First Act.

50

ACT II.

Nº 22. RITORNELLE.

Scene. *The Grove. Enter Æneas, Dido, Belinda, and their train.*

Nº 23. SONG and CHORUS.

52

Nº 24. SONG.

56

№ 25. RECIT.

№ 26. SONG and CHORUS.

60

№ **27**. RECIT.

62

End of the Second Act.

ACT III.

[Scene. *The Ships. Enter the Sailors.*]

Nº 28. PRELUDE [, SONG and CHORUS.]

64

(Enter Sailors.) 1st SAILOR.

Come a - way, fel - low sai - lors, come a - way, Your

an - chors be weigh-ing, Time and tide will ad — mit no— de - lay-ing, Take a

66

№ 29. THE SAILORS' DANCE.

(Enter Sorceress and Witches.)

70

№ 30. RECIT. [and DUET.]

72

SONG.

Moderato.

SORCERESS.

Bass.

Our next mo - tion Must be to storm, _____ her ___ lov-er on the

Basso.

Harpsichord.

Moderato.

o - cean! Our next mo - tion Must be to storm, _____ her

lov-er on the o-cean; From the ru-in of oth-ers Our plea-sures we bor-row, E - lis-sa bleeds

_____ to - night, E - lis - sa bleeds _____ to - night, And Car-thage flames to - mor-row.

№ 31. CHORUS.

74

№ 32. THE WITCHES' DANCE.

78

(Enter Dido, Belinda and Aeneas.)

№ 33. RECIT.

80

82

№ 34. RECIT.

№ 35. CHORUS.

84

№ 36. RECIT.

№ 37. SONG.

-mem-ber me, but ah! for - get___ my fate. Re - mem-ber me, but

ah!_____ for - get my fate.

№ 38. CHORUS.

88

The End.